THE LIGHT SHINES

A collection of poems reflecting a mother's journey through grief

By Stephanie James-Brown
Illustrated by Julia Cross

Published in 2023 by Amazon KDP Publishing.

© 2023 Stephanie James-Brown.

All rights reserved. No part of this publication may be reproduced, copied, stored in a retrieval system, or transmitted, in any form or by any means, without the prior written consent of the copyright holder, nor be otherwise circulated in any form of binding or cover other than that in which it is published and without a similar condition being imposed on the subsequent purchaser.

Cover art by Julia Cross.

All illustrations © 2023 Julia Cross. All rights reserved.

Formatting and copy editing by Naomi Munts Proofreading.

Unless marked otherwise, all Scripture quotations are taken from the Holy Bible, New International Version®, NIV® Copyright ©1973, 1978, 1984, 2011 by Biblica, Inc.® Used by permission. All rights reserved worldwide.

Scripture quotations marked "ESV" are taken from the ESV® Bible (The Holy Bible, English Standard Version®), copyright © 2001 by Crossway, a publishing ministry of Good News Publishers. Used by permission. All rights reserved.

Scripture quotations marked "NLT" are taken from the Holy Bible, New Living Translation, copyright © 1996, 2004, 2015 by Tyndale House Foundation. Used by permission of Tyndale House Publishers, Inc., Carol Stream, Illinois 60188. All rights reserved.

Scripture quotations marked "NKJV" are taken from the New King James Version®. Copyright © 1982 by Thomas Nelson. Used by permission. All rights reserved.

Scripture quotations marked "NASB" are taken from the New American Standard Bible®. Copyright © 1960, 1971, 1977, 1995, 2020 by The Lockman Foundation. All rights reserved.

Scripture quotations marked "HCSB" are taken from the Holman Christian Standard Bible. Copyright © 1999, 2000, 2002, 2003, 2009 by Holman Bible Publishers, Nashville Tennessee. All rights reserved.

Scripture quotations marked "TLB" are taken from the Living Bible, copyright © 1971 by Tyndale House Foundation. Used by permission of Tyndale House Publishers Inc., Carol Stream, Illinois 60188. All rights reserved.

Scripture quotations marked "KJV" are taken from the Bible, King James Version (public domain).

"Enlightening and comforting. These emotional poems reflected my feelings of grief and my tears fell."

—Christine, psychologist

"The lament of love and loss echoes through as Stephanie is held in unseen arms."

—Ursula, nurse

"This collection of poems, reflections and prayers carefully and heartwarmingly captures the rollercoaster of emotions of the bereavement journey and will be a helpful resource for others facing the loss of a loved one. Stephanie openly shares her journey of loss and search for peace."

—Rev. Lee Davies, Parish of Hythe

"This is a beautiful compilation of raw honesty in which love and hope shine through. Along with the beautiful illustrations, I'm sure it will be a source of comfort and solace to many."

—Alison, midwife

"Deeply moving, deeply stimulating. Stephanie speaks honestly of her experience, unafraid to share her raw pain. Stephanie, beautifully, goes through the seasons finding joy and sorrow at every stage with the golden thread of God's love shining through it all."

—Rev. Sue Pitkin, hospital chaplain

In memory of
Peter Ian James Brown
29.04.96–18.06.21

The light shines in the darkness, and the darkness can never extinguish it.

John 1:5 NLT

Contents

PREFACE 11

The Wave of Sorrow 17
Cast Adrift 18
Autumn Leaves 21
In the Silence 22
Part of Me 23
My Birthday 25
Too Much to Bear This Christmas 26
Christmas Day 27
New Year's Day 29
Doing Really Well 30
New Beginnings 32
Fingerprints 34
I Find Your Love 37
We Hold Your Hand 39
Help Me, Lord 41
The River Flows 43
Hold Fast to Love 45
Hatchet Moor 47
Refuge 48
Hands of Prayer 49
One Step Forward 50
Ordinary Things 51
New Paths 53
Fairground Rides 55
Guardian Angels 56
Finding Solace 59
Easter 61
Your Birthday 62
All is Well 64

Praise of Creation	65
Traces	67
Still in the Ocean	68
He's Gone	69
The Dragonfly	71
The Tunnel	73
Rhythm of the Tide	75
Finding Quiet	76
O Still Small Voice of Calm	78
What Is This Life?	79
The Passing of Time	80
Bound for Another Life	82

PREFACE

My son Peter was 25 when he died suddenly on the way back from one of our regular trips to the bottle bank. Well, I say he died then – in truth it was actually about 33 hours later, but it felt like that was when he died, when he slipped into a coma following a heart attack and never woke up. The hospital were wonderful; he had heart surgery and they were kind and attentive, but Peter never came back to us. The following day after the surgery we were told that the damage to his arteries was irreparable and he would likely die from multi-organ failure and further heart attacks. It is true that grief physically hurts. The pain in my heart was intense, and when Peter had the final heart attack at 4 a.m. the next morning, we started our journey of loss.

      Peter was the youngest son, his brother Christopher being almost three years older. Peter was a live wire and was diagnosed with autism in his early years of school. He had a myriad of needs as he grew from childhood to adulthood, and life was a mixture of joys and trials. He suffered from a hearing impairment and from chronic eczema which flared up in his teenage years, and he also developed epilepsy at age 17. Although life was very challenging for Peter at times, he enjoyed so much of it. He was a chatterbox who had a number of special interests that he could talk for hours about. He loved trains and the London Underground, James Bond films and taking things apart. He had a plethora of tools and was always looking to buy more for different projects. He would take apart old washing machines, computers or anything people would give him.

      When he died, life became very quiet and days seemed very empty. Peter's interests and activities had completely filled our days. My world had always revolved around him and the things he liked to do. When you are caring for someone with a disability, it often does. But amidst all this, I also found a peace. A lot of that was found in nature – God's creation. From here my poems were born.

Sometimes it is difficult to say how you feel or for others to know what to say or do with a grieving friend or family member. Sometimes people don't want to mention their name for they are concerned that it will upset you. I hope my poems help people to know that there is no right way to grieve. We are all different and the best thing we can do for each other is simply to be kind to one another. To understand that it's okay to feel deeply sad at times, to cry repeatedly, to have days when you feel numb, days when you don't want to do anything or see anyone, even days when you want to leave this mortal world and join them. But it's also okay to find love and laughter in life, to spend time with friends and family enjoying fun times and chatter, to go on holiday, take up new activities, walk in the countryside and find quiet and stillness in special places.

Peter died on 18 June 2021. It was still COVID times but a driver in a car travelling the same road stopped to help with CPR, offering mouth-to-mouth resuscitation on a stranger. Sadly, we were never able to find him and thank him, as although Peter never regained consciousness, his actions helped to keep Peter alive long enough for him to be transferred to hospital and for our older son to join us in those last hours of Peter's life. I sincerely hope that either he or someone who knows him reads this book and can convey our heartfelt thanks.

Losing Peter left a huge heart-shaped hole that it is difficult to describe, but sadly, that journey of grief was only to deepen, as just eight months later in February 2022, my sister died at the age of 67. She had heart failure but had kept the severity of her condition to herself, and when she went into hospital with a chest infection at the start of the new year, she rapidly declined. She lived just over an hour's drive from me, so in her last weeks I visited regularly, but as her last days drew near, I could no longer watch and wait once again. My sister had six children and between them, they kept a 24-hour vigil round her bed, which I am deeply grateful for, but each had their own memories of joy and regrets which affected their relationships with each other. Families are all different; they fall out and make up and fall out again. We want grief to unite everyone, but everyone grieves differently and sometimes that is not easy, even in the most supportive of families.

After my sister's death, I spent much time visiting my nieces and nephews, helping with funeral arrangements and just spending time with them. Then, just four weeks after my sister's funeral, my mum died. My mum was 93 and had been diagnosed with Alzheimer's at age 89, and steadily her mobility and cognition had declined. She spent the last two years of her life in a care home local to her in Lincolnshire. In truth, the dementia had robbed her of her precious memories some time before and she had no recollection of us, but her death was like losing her all over again. My brother, who had lived with my mum, was bereft, and the next year was punctuated with many journeys to Lincolnshire to support my brother and help him move back south to be nearer to family.

I often ask myself if I ever really grieved my sister and my mum. I'm not sure I did. I'm not even sure when I will. In some ways, I felt frustrated that their deaths had taken away my time to mourn Peter's passing. There had been so little time to grieve solely for him before Sue and Mum died. I constantly remind myself that they are all free from the sufferings of this world. They are all at peace.

This painting is based on a photo that was used to create the wraparound design on Peter's coffin. Peter enjoyed weekly activities with equine therapy and farm services.

Peter died at 4 a.m. on 18 June 2021. That day was filled with phoning family and just sitting together in the shock. The next day, I wrote the following reflection, and that started the journey of *The Light Shines*…

The Wave of Sorrow

Peter has died.

It feels like I am in an ocean,

Trapped within giant waves of sorrow and grief.

Now and then, these waves are interrupted

By a rift of light and cherished memories,

But then the wave of sadness swallows me up once again

And the darkness and inability to breathe within the wave becomes unbearable

And I just have to sit in the wave and let the sadness consume me

Until the light filters through again to give me breath and relief

And the energy to sustain the overwhelming wave of sadness

As it suddenly rises up and swallows me once more.

CAST ADRIFT

There is a numbness,

A disbelief that all is quiet,

He isn't here, he won't be coming back.

I continue with everyday tasks;

Sometimes that's okay, sometimes it isn't.

He is sleeping forever in heaven

And I am bereft.

```
I the Lord your God, will hold your right hand,
   saying to you, "Fear not, I will help you."
                  Isaiah 41:13 NKJV
```

Cast out on a boat in the ocean
With no sail to set a course,
An ocean of waves
But sometimes nothing.
I am just bobbing about
Numb and directionless.
Lord, navigate me through the ocean
And bring me safely to shore.

It's November and I am sitting in the gardens at Romsey Abbey. I find myself watching the trees in the autumn wind.

Autumn Leaves

The tree has leaves still on it,

Leaves that blow in the wind and don't fall to the ground.

Sometimes my sadness and grief is like that;

It won't leave me but clings to me like those leaves cling to the tree.

The wind blows and the rain falls but they still hold on fast,

Refusing to succumb to the autumn call.

But as I look again at those leaves, holding fast to every twig, every branch,

I also see their beauty, their hue of colours.

Each leaf is different and each leaf has a story,

A story of bud and birth, unfolding and becoming a part of the tree's bigger story,

A beautiful story of creation and new life.

Perhaps my grief is like that?

Leaves of memories that hold on fast, and I have to recognise their beauty,

I have to hold onto their hues of colour.

One day, when they're ready, when I'm ready,

They will fall with the wind, but they will never leave,

They will continue on their journey,

They will become and always remain part of that bigger story.

In the Silence

Thank you for sitting with me in the sadness;

Thank you for standing with me in the sadness.

Thank you, special friends, for the quietness,

For not offering words or expressions of comfort,

For just being with me in that moment.

For no words can fill that huge void,

No words can build a bridge over it,

No words can build a path round it,

For there is no way around that huge heart-shaped hole, only through.

Thank you for being with me, silently, quietly on a part of that journey,

Sitting with me in moments of grief,

Offering silence and that safe space.

Moments of silence, of being with thoughts and memories

Help me to move one step forward,

Help me to find peace and joy in treasured memories of togetherness,

Help me to smile,

To know that he will always be with me,

To know that he will always have a special place in my heart.

A friend loves
at all times.

Proverbs 17:17

> It's December and I'm trying to do things to keep myself busy and tell myself 'I'm okay'.

PART OF ME

I can think I'm happy,
Believe that I'm enjoying what I'm doing,
But then suddenly it comes.
It doesn't creep up on me slowly,
It just bites – one big bite from seemingly nowhere.
No reflections, no stirred memories, no real reason;
It just bites, and the pain and anguish cannot be contained.
It rises to the surface, tears flow,
And that deep sense of loss prevails once more.
Does time heal? Does it 'get better'?
Does time bring acceptance?
How can one accept such a huge loss, such overwhelming sorrow?
Perhaps time moulds a new shape.
He was by my side,
A part of me, enabling me to be different things.
Now he is within me.
I am a new shape, absorbing his love and kindness.
He is still a part of me, just no longer clearly visible.

Today is my birthday and I wrote this in the early hours. I couldn't sleep and lay awake thinking about a birthday without Pete and worrying that I couldn't think of any family photos or memories of doing things on my birthday, only the memory of sitting by his bed in intensive care on my last birthday in 2020 when he had sepsis and pneumonia.

He heals the brokenhearted and binds up their wounds.

Psalm 147:3

MY BIRTHDAY

It's my birthday.
I want to share it with you.
I want to share all our birthdays with you.
But there are no more shared celebrations,
No more blowing out candles,
No more eating cake,
Just an empty chair
Where you sang, reluctantly,
Where you enjoyed cake, fervently,
Where you watched me open presents,
Where we ate dinner together,
Where we made memories;
Happy memories,
Not those by a hospital bed.

TOO MUCH TO BEAR THIS CHRISTMAS

I'm tired, and emotional.
Small things bring me to tears,
Even things unconnected to him.
It's like just one more thing is too much to bear,
Too much to bear this Christmas.

I throw myself into things
In the belief that keeping busy will help,
Keeping busy will make Christmas more bearable.
But in truth, now I realise
Keeping busy is wearing me out;
Keeping busy might be too much to bear this Christmas.

The emotional pain is draining me.
I need to rest.
I need to find space for sadness.
Then I will feel God's peace,
Then I will see joy,
Then I will know love,
Then I will find this Christmas.

Come to me, all you who are weary and burdened, and I will give you rest.

Matthew 11:28

CHRISTMAS DAY

"And the light shineth in the darkness."
I hold onto that promise with all my might,
With every fibre of my being,
As today it's Christmas Day… It's 1.30 a.m.
Christmas Eve was difficult, and I fear today.
I have held back tears so much, my head hurts.
I have wanted to cry and wail,
But sometimes you need to be alone to truly wail.
I need to sleep,
To rest in God's peace,
To find his stillness,
To know his hope this Christmas Day,
To remember "The Light will shine in the darkness
And the darkness will not overcome it."
As the sun rises, Lord,
May I feel your presence,
Know your eternal peace,
And may your love shine through me
To those around me.
Amen.

> Blessed are those who mourn,
> for they will be comforted.
>
> Matthew 5:4

New Year's Day

It's New Year's Day.
Another memory,
Another milestone, another 'first',
Another nail in the coffin,
Closing the lid ever tighter,
Shutting that door a bit closer.

I don't like that feeling,
The sadness of the bells striking 2022.
It feels like I'm losing him.
It's no longer the year he died,
Time has moved on,
And with it, people will expect me to move on.

"That was last year, now it's 2022."
But I don't want to move on,
I don't want to put him in a time frame,
Close the door, fasten the box.
I want it forever open.
I want to talk about him,
I want to feel him with me always.

2022 is a new year,
But I still want it to be alive,
Not just with new memories
But cherished memories of him.

I still want to have moments in quiet,
Moments in sadness,
Moments in joy,
And moments of inner peace,
Inner peace that all is well.

I don't have to move on.
I'm there already,
Taking him with me into 2022.
We shall always journey together.
I don't need 'closure'.
I don't have to leave him behind,
I carry him in my heart.

DOING REALLY WELL

"You're doing really well."
"You're amazing."
"You're coping brilliantly."

"You're doing really well."
What does that really mean?
What does 'really well' even look like?

Does it mean you're not a weeping wreck?
Does it mean you've got out of bed and faced the day?
Does it mean you went out and met a friend?

So... what does 'not doing well' look like?
Is it shedding so many tears that your eyes feel sore?
Is it not wanting to get up, get dressed and think 'what next'?
Is it collapsing in a heap looking at old photos, videos,
And smelling his familiar clothes?
Is it avoiding talking about family for fear of loosing that waterfall of grief?
Is it wishing you could join him?

Perhaps 'doing really well' is all of these:
Times of deep sorrow,
Of tears that cannot be held back;
Times of sharing memories with friends;
Times of lying under the duvet alone with your thoughts;
Times of planning a much-loved activity;
Times of quiet and tears in special places;
Times of laughter and looking forward – if only a small step.

Perhaps 'doing really well'
Is knowing that God is by our side,
Taking each small step with us.

I know the Lord is always with me. I will not be shaken, for he is right beside me.

Psalm 16:8 NLT

It's January. The wintry sun has been so bright and the air has been so cold, but daffodils have appeared in the shops. I love daffodils.

Flowers appear on the earth; the season of singing has come, the cooing of doves is heard in our land.

Song of Songs 2:12

New Beginnings

The sun shines but it's cold and wintry,
Frost covers the ground and ice hangs in the air.
But spring is ready to break through:
Daffodils and blossom,
Green shoots and birdsong.

Another season will soon pass,
Another season without you,
And a new one to begin,
Fresh with new beginnings,
New beginnings without you.

But you are here.
You're in the daffodils bursting through the bulb,
You're in the pinkness of the blossom,
You're in the music of the birdsong,
You're in the leaves unfurling on the trees,
You're in the brightness of that wintry sun,
You're in the wonder of that supermoon.
You're in all those special places you loved so much.
Winter is passing,
But you are walking with us into spring.

FINGERPRINTS

When is it time to let go?
To wash the fingerprints off the patio door?
To take the clothes to the charity shop?
To discard the old papers, his wordsearches, timetables...
When is it time?

Six months, twelve months, eighteen months, two years?
When is it time?
To take the bedding off his bed?
To give away all the books, jigsaw puzzles,
To empty the drawers and clear the cupboards?

When is it my time? When is it your time?
Both times are different;
Whose time shall we use?
It's too early for me. It's too late for you.
Whose time shall we use?
There is no right time.

Little things, one piece at a time,
That's all I can do.
One book here, one puzzle there,
Two coats to there, two shoes to there,
That's all I can do right now.

Not even a year.

I still want him here, around me.

One piece at a time,

In my time.

There is no right time.

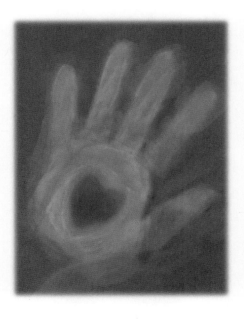

I wrote this whilst sitting at a special place at Hatchet Moor, where I love to go and be surrounded by nature. It reminds me of Beth Neilson's song "I find your love in everything", which we played at Peter's funeral.

I Find Your Love

The peace
And the stillness,
The winter sunset
Against a blue sky.

The ripples on the water,
The reflection of the trees,
The wind through the leaves,
What few there are.

The floss of the clouds,
The sounds of the ducks,
The fragility of the moorhen,
The strength of the rook.

You are here, with all of these.
"I find your love in everything."

It's 26 January and I can't sleep. My sister is very ill. I went to the hospital today with her sons and daughters. COVID restrictions meant we were only permitted to go in twos to sit with her and hold her hand. As we took it in turns to sit with her, we gathered together at the hospital café.

WE HOLD YOUR HAND

I see you,
I hear you,
I hold your hand
Amongst the noise
And bustle of hospital life.

Within clinical corridors
And coffee shops
We talk,
We share memories,
We prepare ourselves
For your passing.

But it is a bitter pill to swallow,
A life not lived to the full,
Recent years of pain and sadness.

But we try
To prepare ourselves,
To share love,
To share kindness,
To support each other
In these fragile moments.
We see you,
We hear you.

We look for hope,
We treasure each smile,
We hang on each word.
Please stay with us,
We're not ready to lose you.

Once again we hold your hand,
We tell you we love you,
We tell you we'll see you soon.
We walk towards the door
Past beeping machines,
Down clinical corridors,
Past the coffee shop
And into the light.

And one day, very soon,
You will walk towards the light,
You will see the Son,
You will be free from suffering.
But for now, just for now,

We see you,
We hold your hand,
We treasure your smile.

For he will command his angels concerning
you to guard you in all your ways.

Psalm 91:11

Help Me, Lord

(A prayer for my sister as she passes in February 2022)

Help me, Lord.

I don't know how I'm going to get through the next day, the next week, the next month.

Right now, I don't even know how I'll get through the next eight hours.

I can't sleep, I'm so worried about her.

I want her to know how much she is loved, how much she has always been loved.

Sometimes I worry that she might not know that,

That she might not have felt the depth of that love.

I want her to feel it now.

I want her to feel wrapped in love, as warm and soft as a cosy blanket.

I want her to know your peace, your perfect peace.

I want her to feel the presence of your guardian angels, gently touching and blessing her and making her feel safe.

I don't want to lose her but I know we will;

I don't want to let her go but I know we have to.

Help her Lord, take hold of her hand

And guide her towards your light.

When it's time, Lord, may she leave us peacefully,

Knowing that she is surrounded by love.

Amen.

My sister died on 11 February, another loss so soon after Peter.
I wrote this as I sat in the war memorial park in Romsey watching
the river.

THE RIVER FLOWS

The river flows

Like streams of tears on a cold grey day.

The trees sway silently

As if they know quiet is needed,

Space and time with thoughts and memories.

It is a shared grief;

We all loved her,

We all wish we had said it more.

Spring is coming,

But this year you won't see the blossom;

But we will see it for you,

We will hold each flower, each petal,

And we will remember you,

We will remember your smiles

And share your laughter.

Tears may flow,

But we will see the sun shine,

For you will bring light to that cold grey day.

The river flows,

The trees sway,

An oasis of peace in a busy world.

> The earth is the LORD's, and all it contains.
>
> Psalm 24:1 NASB

Death of a loved one brings such differing emotions. My sister had a big family and each grieve in their own ways. I visit Peter's grave to talk to him about the sorrow and struggles of his cousins and then return to the car, parked by the wetlands at Eling Tide Mill, and write this.

HOLD FAST TO LOVE

The sun is setting,

The birds flying home.

I watch, silently,

As the bulrushes dance in the breeze

And creation settles to an evening rest.

The peace is my tonic,

A haven of quiet within chaotic moments.

As the setting sun stirs differing activity,

So grief stirs different emotions:

Sadness, regret, anger and love.

We cling to the love,

But the grief peers through,

And grief disguises itself

In harsh words, tarnished memories.

But hold fast,

Hold fast to the love;

Don't let the anger carry you,

For it will trap you,

It will destroy you,

It will separate you from love.

Hold fast to love;

It will carry you home.

> A gentle answer turns away wrath,
> but a harsh word stirs up anger.
>
> Proverbs 15:1

Mother's Day is approaching and my grief is profound and heightened by the loss of Sue too. It's my first Mother's Day without Peter, and I feel the loss creeping into my bones again. Some people react to me as though the grief of losing a child with special needs is not so great, as if now I have been released from a burden of care and am free to get on with my life, but in truth the grief is no less, as Peter was such a huge part of my life every day. I need to cry in my own space, so I go to Hatchet Moor again, my special place in the forest, listening to nature and the still small voice of God.

HATCHET MOOR

Bottoms up are the swans and the ducks,
Pitter patter is the rain on the windscreen,
Caw, caw says the gull on the gravel,
Whoo, whoo is the wind in the trees,
And "All is well" says my God in heaven.

REFUGE

My loss is great,

My burden weighs heavy,

But in you I trust.

You are my refuge,

My shelter from the storm.

Without you I am just noise,

But with you my spirit can fly.

> God is our refuge and strength,
> a very present help in trouble.
>
> Psalm 46:1 NKJV

Russia has invaded Ukraine. Peter always felt so strongly about war and conflict. Each Sunday, we would say a simple prayer at dinner time and he would always pray for those in conflict situations.

HANDS OF PRAYER

I miss your voice.

I miss the conversations we used to have,

Your endless chatter,

Your presence.

Life is quiet now.

I sit by your grave,

I listen to the birds,

I bring you another flower.

Today it's a primula – blue and yellow for Ukraine.

You would want to support them,

To pray for them.

I will do that for you.

Yes, I shall be your voice.

I shall be your voice that delights in the sight of a train passing,

I shall be your hands that give food to the ducks,

I shall be your ears that listen to the crash of glass at the bottle bank,

I shall be your eyes that marvel at the sunset and the moon,

I shall be your heart that gives love to those in need.

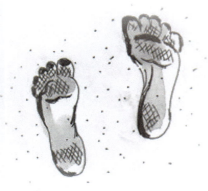

> ...it was then that I carried you.
>
> *Footprints in the Sand* by M. Stevenson

ONE STEP FORWARD

I watch the clock
As I think of you,
I listen to the sounds around me
As I think of you,
I lie here in the dark as I think of you.
I'm like the buoy in the ocean,
Bobbing up and down with the current.
Numb, I cannot sleep.
It is true, you have gone;
I cannot see you, I cannot touch you.
I talk to you, I tell you things,

But you cannot talk back.
You smile at me from your photo,
A smile that conveys a thousand words,
A smile that tells me you're okay.
I smile back.
I tell you some days I am lost,
Lost on that ocean.
Who am I now?
And that still small voice
Says, "One step forward..."
One step forward.

ORDINARY THINGS

I take out the washing,
I hang it on the drier;
I think of you.

I think of you helping,
Hanging up your socks
And chatting to me;
I miss those chats.

Not just a little... I miss them a lot.

I think about things we used to do:
Feeding the ducks, a trip to the shops,
Recycling, visiting places;
I miss those things.

Not just a little... I miss them a lot.

The house will be quiet soon,
Just me and Dad,
Weekly chores and coffee in the conservatory.
I will think of you,
I will miss you.

Not just a little... I will miss you a lot.

Our son and his girlfriend moved in with us after Peter's funeral, whilst they were looking at places to buy. It has buffered the quietness for us by their activity and chatter, but now they are moving out into their own home.

You reveal the path of life to me; in Your presence is abundant joy; in Your right hand are eternal pleasures.

Psalm 16:11 HCSB

New Paths

The boxes are packed,
The van is gone,
The goodbyes have been said,
And I'm here with my memories.

I walk into each room;
My emotions are mixed,
Of sadness and joy,
Of doors closing and doors opening.

A new journey,
A new adventure,
Not only for you
But for me, for us too.

Spring brings new life,
Blossoms of hope,
New paths to explore;
But for now
I'm here with my memories.

My mum passed away on 5 April. She was 93. Although I have a peace about it, I am exhausted, reliving my grief for Peter through each death – my sister and now Mum. There is so much still to do, family that need support.

FAIRGROUND RIDES

I feel like I'm on a waltzer.
I really want to sit quiet and still,
But everything is spinning around me,
So fast that I can hardly see it or grasp it.

I want to get off.
I've been on this ride for too long.
I'm dizzy, tired, worn out, exhausted.
I want to help,
But I'm spinning too fast;
I'm losing control of me… Of ME…
Who am I?
Someone's aunt, someone's sister?
Where am I?
Where is Me?

I need you all to go away
Just for a little while,
Just to give me time,
Time to find me, to be Me.
I love you,
But please understand
I've been on this ride too long;
I need quietness,
I need to be still.

GUARDIAN ANGELS

Mum has passed
Peacefully into the night,
Leaving us memories,
Holding us tight.

Sue has left us,
A family alone,
Grieving children,
An empty home.

Peter's in heaven
Holding God's hand,
Asking him questions,
Footprints in sand.

Footprints in sand
Is where I shall be;
Too tired to walk,
Jesus carries me.

Losing three family
In less than a year,
Three generations,
So many tears.

Guardian angels
Holding each one;
Peter, Sue, Mum,
At home with the Son.

> Behold, I send an angel before you to guard you on the way and to bring you to the place that I have prepared.
>
> Exodus 23:20 ESV

Finding Solace

Sleeping is difficult again.
My brain is buzzing
Like current through a power cable.

So many things to do,
To remember, to think about;
Finding calm, finding stillness
Is difficult.

I want to sleep.
I need to sleep.
But I can't turn my brain off;
I can't switch the power off
And rest.

It's just constantly buzzing,
Morning, noon and night,
A meter racing on,
Clocking up digits,
Running up a debt
It cannot pay off.

My only solace is in you, Lord,
To rest in your peace,
To linger in your garden,
To listen to the birds,
To watch the trees,
To find your stillness
In the praise of creation.

Only with you, Lord,
Can I harness the power,
Capture it, work with it,
For your power is made perfect
In my weakness.

Lord, help me to keep you at the centre.
Help my scrambled thoughts
To find clarity in your hands;
Help my sleepless spirit
To find rest in your arms;
Help my tired heart
To find love in your embrace.

I am the resurrection and the life. The one who believes in me will live, even though they die.

John 11:25

EASTER

Easter passed.
There was no egg hunt,
No laughter searching
For hidden treasures,

No smiles of joy
At chocolate boxes,
Savouring mouthfuls
Of sweet treats,

No cakes with mini eggs,
No James Bond films,
No things to take apart.

Easter came.
The Son rose –
The promise of resurrection –
And I thought of you,
Safe in God's embrace.

Your Birthday

It's your birthday.
You would be 26.
I would make a cake.
There would be presents:

A James Bond DVD,
Some tools,
And chocolate,
Always some chocolate.

We would do something,
Go somewhere.
But not today;
Not any day.

How best shall we remember you?
How shall we celebrate
Your life, this day?

A walk? Photographs? Memories in quiet?

How best can we remember
Such a cherished life
When sadness rolls in
Over unaccomplished adventures?

Of things we said we'd do,
Places we said we would go,
Adventures we never
Had a chance to complete.

How shall we remember you, this special day?

We will remember you with love,
With smiles, with joy,
Of the things we did do.

The cherished memories
Of special moments.
We will remember
You are free,
And in your freedom
We will find our peace.

> They are like trees along a riverbank bearing luscious fruit each season without fail. Their leaves shall never wither, and all they do shall prosper.
>
> Psalm 1:1–3 TLB

ALL IS WELL

People live and people die,
But in between
There is a cacophony of noise
And a symphony of melody.

I miss you all
In different ways,
Ways that words
Cannot always express,
But creation echoes your love,
Your kindness, your strength.

In creation, I find your heartbeat,
I hear your symphony,
I see your footprints
Paving the way.

I hear your whisper in the trees,
"All is well" echoing back to me.
All is well.

Praise of Creation

I feel your presence here, Lord,

In the gentle wind of the Holy Spirit dancing in the trees,

In the praise of the daffodils as their golden glow bows to the heavens,

In the song of the birds raising a melody to creation,

In the quiet moment that whispers,

"Be still and know that I am God."

Let everything that has breath
praise the Lord.

Psalm 150:6

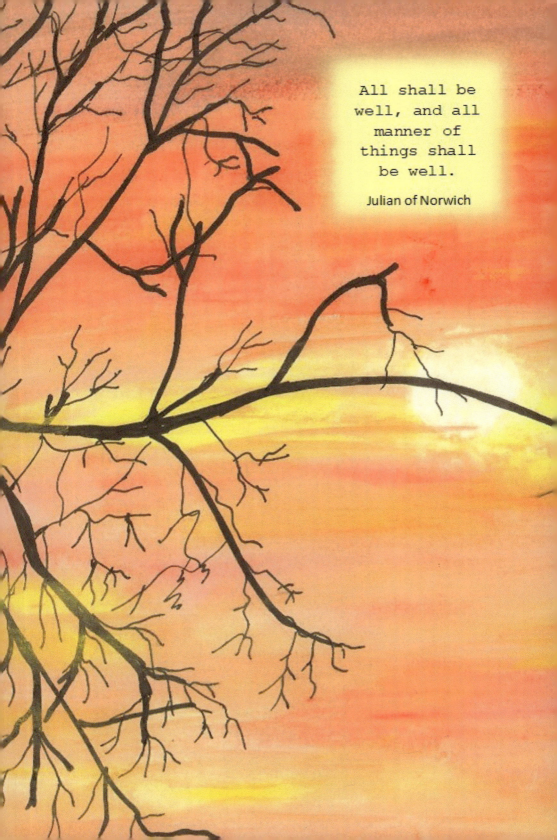

TRACES

I feel so sad,
And no one can really understand my sadness.
I see your favourite duvet cover,
I dust your photo;
I listen for your voice,
But all is quiet
Except for birdsong.

Dusting is poignant.
I come across traces of you
Everywhere:
Small keys, puzzle pieces,
And photos... lots of photos.

I listen for your voice,
But all is quiet
Except for birdsong.

I worry I will not remember
Your voice,
Your chatter,
Your laughter.
But in the quiet I hear you,
In the birdsong, you sing
All is well, all is well.

It's June, the month Peter died, and as the anniversary of his death gets closer, my sadness increases. I cycle to the little local slipway and watch the tide going out.

STILL IN THE OCEAN

I'm sad,
So sad.
There is nothing to say,
Only that I am sad.
Being here
Watching the tide helps.
I remember being in that ocean last year.
Perhaps now the ocean is not so vast,
Not so turbulent,
Not so painful;
But it still hurts.
The waves don't swallow me so deeply
For so long,
But they still engulf me.
I still have to hold my breath
As another one rises up,
Especially now,
Especially as we approach
The day you died.

Today is the anniversary of Pete's death, and I am feeling it even more strongly this week as I have COVID and cannot do the things I wanted to do to remember Peter and celebrate his life. I started this poem but didn't finish it.

HE'S GONE

It's not all right,
It will never be all right.
He's gone,
I'll never see him again,
I'll never hear his voice again.
How can it ever be all right?
How could I ever not be sad?

When would it ever not be sad?
There will always be sadness,
But there will always be light too.
We need them both.
There is no joy without tears,
For in the sadness we feel the most…

Weeping may endure for a night, but joy cometh in the morning.

Psalm 30:5 KJV

It's July, and I decide to spend the day at Exbury Gardens. I sit by the dragonfly pond and am reminded of the story the minister told at the Holy Innocents service at Romsey Abbey in January. I write this poem.

THE DRAGONFLY

Was your life like the dragonfly?
Struggling underneath before climbing the iris,
Then set free in the sunshine,
Free to fly,
To experience the world?
But not for ever,
Not for long:
Moments of joy,
Moments of wonder,
Moments of pain,
Moments of blessings,
Short lived,
Gone too soon,
Barely enough time to spread your wings,
To find your way in this chaotic world.
But you have flown now
And left us for another world.
Spread your wings, young emperor,
Let your colour glisten in the sun,
Let your song ripple over the pond.
Fly free and know
That one day I will fly with you.

Peter loved train rides. I take the train at Exbury Gardens and write this poem.

THE TUNNEL

Is that how it was for you
On that fateful day?
Like entering a tunnel,
A moment consumed by darkness
Before entering the light?
How long did it take to see the light?
How long did it take to recognise the angels?
To feel the Spirit,
To know God's love
As his arms embraced you on the other side?
Bathe in the love, my child,
And know you are always close at heart.

I return to the little local slipway for time alone with my thoughts on life moving forward.

RHYTHM OF THE TIDE

The fish are swimming in the shallows.
They will go out again with the tide
And they will come back in again,
Part of a regular rhythm,
Life's regular rhythm.
Mine has changed,
But theirs continues.
Everything around me continues.
People go off to work,
They walk their dogs,
They chat together in busy cafés.
I want to stop them and tell them you died,
I want to say how much I miss you,
But that rhythm stops me.
Life continues,
Each minute, each hour, each day, each week.
Life continues,
The rhythm flows like the tide,
Our hearts beat to a new tune.

FINDING QUIET

I can find you here, God,

Sitting in creation.

I can find you in the space,

In the quietness,

In the wind,

In the purple heather moving in the breeze.

Sometimes it's difficult at home,

Sometimes it's difficult to find you in relationships,

The stress and strain of finding new ways to be alone

And new ways to be together.

But here I find you.
Here the quietness drowns out the loud voices
And fills the spaces with hope and love.
Here I feel free to be... just me.

Cast all your anxiety on him
because he cares for you.

1 Peter 5:7

> The Lord bless you and keep you; the Lord make his face to shine upon you and be gracious to you; the Lord lift up his countenance upon you and give you peace.
>
> Numbers 6:24–26 ESV

O Still Small Voice of Calm

O still small voice of calm
In the quietness of this day,
In the patterns that we weave,
In the love along the way,
In the air we breathe so freely,
In the dawn and to the dusk,
In the sunsets and sunrises
We hear your voice of love.
We may not see your face,
We may not feel your touch,

But your smile is in the faces
Of those we love so much.
Your touch is in the help
Given by others' hands,
Your voice is in the words
Of those who help us stand,
Who take us from dark places
And raise us up to praise,
Who encourage us to trust
There will be brighter days.

What Is This Life?

O what is this life, if I tread carefully,

If I avoid the challenges

And skip the adventures?

O what is this life

If I am just content to be

And not to do?

O what is this life

If I wish only to talk

And not to listen?

O what is this life

If I stay in the comfortable

And walk away from the journey?

Trust in the Lord with all thine heart; and lean not unto thine own understanding. In all thy ways acknowledge him, and he shall direct thy paths.
Proverbs 3:5–6 KJV

THE PASSING OF TIME

The passing of time does not make things easier;
I still feel your loss, especially at this time of year.
It is our second Christmas without you,
And the grief still cuts through like an icy wind.

I think about happy memories and force a smile,
But still the grip of that winter chill holds me fast,
Like a wolf's howl of unaccomplished dreams,
An echo through the forest that reminds me you are gone.

The tree shines brightly adorned with decorations,
The Christmas table bears a feast,
The presents sit wrapped under the tree,
But there is an empty space, a silence, unspoken words.

I lie in bed, thinking, crying, gripped by that icy sorrow,
Wondering if tomorrow will be different,
If next year will be different,

Wanting to see you, to hold you, to tell you I love you,
To tell you I'm trying but Christmas can't be the same.
I don't want to do Christmas anymore, not like this.
I don't want to sit here with presents round the tree,
Preparing sumptuous feasts.
I want it to be different now.

I love you, I miss you.
I want to loosen that icy grip,
I want to feel your love around me,
Not in presents, not in feasting,
But in the reflection of your kindness and joy on the faces of others.

Time passes as it always will,
But sorrow doesn't, it remains quite still.
It clings and grips
And holds on tight
And shields itself from glowing light.

I am setting off for Bradford-on-Avon for another funeral –
'Auntie Donnie' who was my auntie Audrey's sister-in-law.
She was 94 years old and no direct relation, but like Audrey, she
shared my faith. Her funeral was just hours after the funeral of our
Queen Elizabeth II.

BOUND FOR ANOTHER LIFE

We are all souls bound for another life,
Beings walking towards our God.
For some, the journey is short,
For others it is long.
You are in good company;
Many kind souls go before you,
Many light the way;
The known and the unknown sing praises,
They rejoice with the angels
As you take each step forward.
Cherished lives
Missed by many,
Safe in the arms of God,
You have found peace.

And I heard a loud voice from the throne saying, "Behold, the dwelling place of God is with man. He will dwell with them, and they will be his people, and God himself will be with them as their God."
Revelation 21:3 ESV

Printed in Great Britain
by Amazon